House Inspection 101
12 Things to Check Before Buying

© 2024

Contents

Chapter 1: What They Don't Tell Homebuyers

So, you are about to sign off on a house, putting your signature on the line for the house and a likely loan that is the biggest loan most people will ever take out. Hold on before you sign! Yes, I understand you more than likely had the house inspected, which is pretty much a standard requirement especially for those getting a loan. Yet, even inspections don't reveal everything! I learned that the hard way.

We purchased our home in the early 2000s. Now, nearly 20 years later, I am overwhelmed by all the things I wish I had asked when I purchased our single-family home. Don't get me wrong, the inspector did a thorough job while the house's previous owner maintained the property well. Yet, all these years later, I still wish I had asked very important questions that would have saved me time and money later on. That's the whole point of this guide. I want readers to have the insight I didn't all those years ago. I kept this guide short, to the point, and inexpensive so as many people as possible could learn from my mistakes.

My Top Recommendation: *Be present when your Inspector inspects the house you are looking to* *buy. Ask questions, and ask the Home Inspector what things you should be looking out for in each room, especially in rooms with plumbing fixtures and major appliances. Also ask for estimates of how long to expect each appliance to last after you buy the house (furnace, AC unit, dryer, washing machine, and fridge).*

Home Ownership 101: Tools and Services

In addition to the tips detailed in this book, I wanted to give readers a list of tools and services to investigate and acquire before buying a home. Let's face facts, all houses have issues or require repairs and maintenance periodically. Well, what if you need to repair a window at 2am? Hey, it happens. So, with that fear now stuck in your mind, here are my recommendations for "must have" services and tools to have in place by the time you sign-off and move into your new home. These are the tools I found most crucial to maintaining my home for 19+ years, especially when catastrophe strikes.

1) ***Service Providers Contact List.*** From inspections and maintenance of utility fixtures (furnace, AC, etc.) to emergency services needed during or after a storm

damages your home, it's a great idea to already have service providers checked out. Trust me, you don't want to have to research trained and trustworthy plumbers while your sinks are clogged or your toilet is backed up. To be honest, I am a huge fan of putting in place a service contract with a local company that handles plumbing, heating, and cooling issues. Sure, it may cost you anywhere from $15 to $100 per month for a service contract, but the first time you have an emergency will make you glad you have the service company on board. The reason why is that such service contracts often include a policy where you are prioritized over customers without a service contract. So, in the event of a weather catastrophe, where most homes in an area are damaged by a storm or flood, those with service contracts get their homes repaired first. On top of that, service contracts often include a reduced rate for any parts/labor required to address a plumbing, heating, or cooling issue.

2) ***Screwdriver Set.*** A typical house has countless appliances, wall fixtures, and other things that are secured by screws. For that reason, make sure you have a basic set of 6-

12 screwdrivers (half Phillips head and half slotted. Additionally, and trust me on this, spend $5 to $15 and get a 'precision' screwdriver set. It's amazing how many everyday items require a tiny screwdriver bit for removing tiny screws. We are talking eye glasses, watches, flashlights, and other tools throughout the home.

3) ***A Bag of Tape.*** Yes, I said a bag, because there are a variety of tapes you need as a homeowner… beyond scotch and masking tape. At all times, homeowners should have a good supply of duct tape, painter's tape, and electrical tape (in addition to the aforementioned scotch and masking tapes). In my experience, having 2 rolls of duct tape is ideal. Likewise, you should consider a roll of packing tape as it is a very durable tape that I found comes in handy in emergencies.

4) ***Hammer Time.*** For all homeowners, a 16oz claw hammer is a true staple that will get used over and over again. From hammering in or removing nails to knocking out drywall in an emergency, a claw hammer is a must. I also suggest a 3 to 6lb sledge hammer if you can afford it. A sledge is a nice friend to have in emergency situations.

5) **Hacksaw.** True, having a small to medium sized hand saw is a good thing to have on hand, but a hacksaw is truly important. From cutting car exhaust pipes that wrap around your car's axel (don't ask) to cutting through nails and many other types of metal, a hacksaw is vital in situations that you can't yet imagine. Make sure you have a compact hacksaw at the minimum, and keep one in the trunk of your car. It's amazing how often hacksaws save the day when on a road trip.

6) **Two Drills.** I know that seems odd, but hear me out. A typical power drill is a great thing to have. Whether corded or battery-powered, a drill can be equipped with a variety of bits that turn your drill into a screwdriver, a sander, or even a plumbing snake. That's on top of serving as a drill. That said, what happens if the power is out and you need a drill? For those situations, make sure you have a hand-powered drill. You can get a good one for around $20-$25 at a hardware store. Oh… and get a variety pack of drill bits or else the drills are just paperweights.

7) **Plunger and Hand Snake.** A plunger to deal with toilet clogs in emergency situations. I

think that's rather self-explanatory. That said, having spoken with friends who worked in plumbing, plungers can damage plumbing systems due to the pressure they generate. Worse, apparently, are the chemical plumbing aids available. I have been informed by certified plumbers that such additives/chemicals are highly corrosive to pipes and piping fixtures. Check out YouTube for videos of the damage chemicals do to pipes and the plunger concerns plumbers have. A basic plumbing snake is the choice preferred by plumbers I spoke with, which are items you can get for around $20. For toilet clogs, check out 'closet augers' for an option.

8) ***Reciprocating Saw.*** Homeowners see a lot of crazy stuff, usually wall supports, framing, and pipe fixtures covered up by previous owners. For many of these situations, cutting the crap out is the best option. Yet, many of these circumstances pop up in tight spaces that are not easily accessible by a hand saw or hacksaw. For such situations, a reciprocating saw comes in handy. You can get a corded-electric (generic brand) reciprocating saw for under $50. It's one of

the more expensive tools you will ever buy, but it's amazing how often these saws save the day.

9) ***Wrenches, Pliers, and Sockets.*** A basic socket and wrench/pliers set is a must for working on everything from plumbing and cars to bicycles and appliances. As for wrenches, make sure you get 2 slip-joint pliers, an adjustable wrench, a needle-nosed pliers, and a lineman's pliers. You should be able to purchase a good socket set for $20 and a combo set of wrenches and pliers for another $20.

10) ***Extension Cords.*** I'm not talking about those thin extension cords you get in most larger grocery stores. Get a HEAVY DUTY extension cord that can handle a minimum of 15 amps. This is important for later. Get one at least 50 feet in length. If your driveway is longer than 50 feet, get an extension cord that is between 75 and 100 feet in length.

11) ***Electric Snow Blower.*** Obviously this one is for areas that get snow. My driveway is 80 feet long... and I live in Buffalo, New York. As I am older and worked some side jobs, I eventually was able to save up and buy a gas-powered snow blower to handle all manner

of snow. So, what happens if your beast of a snow blower stops working during a blizzard or even a regular snowfall? Or, what if a storm goes on for days and you are not able to go to the gas station to buy gasoline? Corded-electric snow blowers are amazingly tough. I purchased a refurbished one on Ebay for under $100 as a backup. Now, two years in a row, that corded-electric snow blower has saved me from shoveling when issues popped up with my gas-powered snow blower. Gas and battery-powered snow blowers, in my experience, have more starting issues and require a good amount of maintenance. Corded-electric need little maintenance. Sure, if power goes out, you're in trouble. Thing is, for areas that get hammered with snow, we usually still have power. Usually. Oh, as for the heavy duty extension cord I mentioned earlier, appliances like electric snow blowers need the heavier gauge extension cords so the cords don't burn out and become a hazard. By the way, I recommend you get a spare auger belt for the snow blower... just in case.

12)　　**_Measuring Tape._** People seem to overlook the importance of exact measurements all the time. Whether you're measuring space available for a dishwasher or measuring a window's dimensions, exact measurements are critical for homeowners. My recommendation? Get two 25 foot measuring tapes with both metric and inch measuring systems.

13)   *Level.* From hanging pictures to putting up shelves, making sure things are 'level' is important. A 9-inch torpedo level is a good place to start.

14)   *Basic Hardware Set.* Nut, bolts, screws, and nails all come into play when owning and maintaining a house. I recommend an assortment (set) of nuts, bolts, screws, and washers that can be purchased at most hardware stores. From there, buy a box of assorted hardware nails. In total, you're probably going to spend around $15-$20.

15)   *Plastic Ties.* I use plastic ties in place of nuts/bolts for securing my mailbox as they tend to hold up better against snow thrown by the town plows (and the ties don't rust). From there, there are countless ways in which a homeowner needs to secure a tarp, electrical cords, or some other home fixture for whatever reason, which is when ties

come in handy. Just have an assortment on hand.

16)   ***Tarps and Plastic Sheeting.*** From broken windows to lawn furniture, homeowners often face a moment, usually during bad weather, when they need to cover something in order to protect it from rain, snow, or some other weather element. The sheeting also comes in handy when covering furniture before painting a room. For a minimum, I advise getting a 8'x6' tarp and a roll of 3mm-thick sheeting (10'x25').

17)   ***Wood.*** As a homeowner, you will experience extreme weather and human error that leads to structural issues. In those instances, a temporary fix (like covering a shattered window) may be needed while waiting hours or days for a repairman to arrive and fix the damage. For such emergencies, I recommend all homeowners have a couple sheets of plywood on hand along with four to six 2'x4's.

18)   ***Shovels.*** A set of shovels actually. One round shovel for digging in the dirt, a snow shovel for … snow, and a garden trowel for maintaining house plants or planting seeds in a garden.

19)   ***Scraper Set.*** Whether plastic or metal, scrapers come in handy when painting or repairing drywall. These relatively inexpensive tools help with removing old residue such as paint or plaster as well as in removing excess putty and plaster when conducting wall repairs.

20)   ***Wet/dry Vac***. Commonly referred to as "Shop-vacs" in reference to one of the major brands, these vacuums are lifesavers for cleaning up after home projects and/or removing water that pops up in basements during and after storms. Regular vacuum cleaners are generally not suited for picking up water. Wet/dry vacs, meanwhile, are a quick way to manage water spills or flooding that pops up from time to time.

21)   ***Two Flashlights***. Sure, mini flashlights are convenient, but I want you to get two hearty flashlights that can really light up a room. When working or searching in the basement during a power outage, you will be glad to have a good flashlight. My father in law likes the heavy duty lights like what security guards carry. My Dad liked those big lantern lights. Both are great options.

CRAIG'S LIST AND HOME PARTIES

First-time homebuyers are often younger adults just starting off in life, whether newly married or just starting off in their career of choice. As a result, these homebuyers often do not have a lot of extra dollars available with which to buy the recommended tools and supplies. In consideration of that, I suggest two alternate ways to obtain/afford the tools listed above. First... check out your local Craig's List.

It's amazing how much you can buy on Craig's List or even at garage sales. If money is tight, making it impossible to buy all new tools, check out Craig's List, garage sales, and flea markets for the tools you need. Such outlets could save you 50% or more off of buying the tools brand new at a store. The one glitch here is that certain tools, especially power tools, won't have as long of a life compared to brand new equivalents. A used drill or reciprocating saw bought at a garage sale could quit in years or in a matter of days. It's a crap shoot. That said, you should get a decent amount of use before you have to get a replacement. Now for the party idea.

When you buy a house, and you are not a multi-millionaire, consider throwing a party to celebrate your new home. Ask guests to bring a meal to pass or a bag of chips along with a tool from the list above. Then, get the grill going, cook up hotdogs and hamburgers and show friends and family the house. The tools they bring will save you money while helping to strengthen your ties with those you love. As an added bonus, such a gathering may reveal a friend or family member who is good at a skill you'll need down the road such as carpentry, electrical repairs, roofing, plumbing, or painting.

IMPORTANT TIP:

In preparation of inspecting a home, check out tips and strategies listed online, especially guidance on things often "hidden" by home sellers, usually with fresh construction or new coats of paint. Check out checklists and tips provided by certified home inspectors online (see YouTube for some options – I recommend you make sure the tips/videos are provided by inspectors certified by national and/or international home inspection associations like the International Association of Certified Home Inspectors).

Chapter 2: Shutoffs – What Turns Off What?

Homes come with a ton of switches. The frustrating thing is that oftentimes, a switch is no longer connected to any specific light as the previous home owner removed the corresponding electrical wiring. Another thing is there are oftentimes lights placed inside the house or outside for which there doesn't appear to be a switch for turning the light on and off.

The home I purchased had outside lights EVERYWHERE! On top of that, the previous owner had installed a pool with a deck and a gas heater. This proved to be a complicated mess the first year I shut down the pool for the winter. The deck for the pool had a buried electrical power line in addition to a gas line. Learning the various shut off switches in the garage was an experience to say the least. I was fortunate that the previous owner had made me aware of where different turn-offs were. I just wish I had been more focused on that when I purchased the house. That said, here are my recommendations regarding shut-offs:

1) ***Power Box Labelling.*** Most power boxes are in the basement of the house. Find out where it is first. From there, look to see what appliances, rooms, and other stuff is listed. You are looking for the shut-offs for the

house's electricity so if a circuit breaker is tripped or repairs need to be made, you know which breaker to flip. For older homes with fuse boxes, you likewise want to find the location of the power box. Oh, in regards to the 2 flashlights I recommended you get, one is meant to be dedicated to getting to the power box during a power outage. You can't flip breakers or change fuses if you can't see the power box. As for labeling, the power box should clearly mark which breaker links to each room in the house as well as the major appliances. If not labeled, ask the homeowner for guidance. In the event the previous homeowner has no clue which circuit breaker turns of what, one of the first things you should do after taking ownership of the home is to identify which circuit breaker connects to each room and major appliance. See if the House Inspector can assist. If an emergency happens to a room or appliance, you want to be able to shut off power immediately without having to shut down power to the whole house.

2) ***Gas Line.*** For homes with gas or those heated by oil, find out where the gas line enters the home and where the shut-off is located. For those with homes heated by oil, ask for guidance from the Home Inspector regarding

maintenance and operation of the furnace if you are unfamiliar with the technology. I recognize that this is pretty straightforward, but it helps to know in case of an emergency where to shut off the gas entering the home. What complicates things further is if gas lines were added by the previous owner(s). In my situation, the home I purchased had gas lines going to both the garage (for a heater) and the pool deck (for the gas-fueled heater). Know how to shut off gas to those lines without having to shut off gas to the main house. In line with that, if the previous owner buried gas lines to outdoor structures, find out where those gas lines are. Why? If you need to dig up your yard in the coming years to install a pool or garage, you want to know where gas (and electrical) lines were buried. Yes, I recommend you have your utilities (and buried lines) be mapped out by utility companies when buying your home. That said, some home owners do unique things when burying gas and electrical lines. For that reason, ask the homeowner about such buried lines. By the way, make sure you install new carbon monoxide detectors throughout your home. Just do it. It's a silent killer you want to protect yourself from.

3) ***Water Main.*** Find where the water main enters the home and where the main shut-off for water is. If a pipe bursts during the winter or if you need to fix a leaking faucet, you'll need to know where the main shut-off is.

Chapter 3: Where are the Water Spigots?

The previous owner of my home did an amazing job in upgrading the house and maintaining records that included user manuals for appliances and the receipts for each major appliance. He also installed a turtle pond in the yard, which my wife turned into a vegetable garden as the turtles were removed before we bought the house. Let me tell you, taking care of turtles seems labor intensive. One thing I learned is how important sinks are to those who own and take care of turtles. Aside from the bathroom and kitchen, my home included multiple sinks in the basement, a sink in the garage, and a sink on the deck. This meant I had a lot of water lines coming and going. Unfortunately, this led to one of my biggest mistakes as a homeowner.

Water spigots. I counted three when we moved in. When winter approached, I shut off the water lines to the auxiliary spigots while the main had no shut-off other than the shut-off to the water main. For that spigot, we capped it with an insulator and eventually had a plumber install a shut-off. That winter, I felt all set. Unfortunately, I overlooked a spigot hidden in a flower garden the previous owner had put in. Because I didn't know it was there, I didn't open the spigot and drain any water remaining in the line before the first freeze.

Well, the water line burst at some point during the winter. As a result, when I turned the water back on in the Spring, water gushed out of the busted pipe immediately. I fortunately realized the problem immediately and shut off the water line. Given the confined space under the deck where the busted pipe was, I had a hell of a time doing a repair. When you buy a home, ask about where all the spigots and water lines are. Then, make sure to know where the shut-offs are for each spigot.

Chapter 4: Sump Pumps and Water Issues

Many homeowners fear water, and I get why. Water can cause significant damage to your home and property, often leading to thousands of dollars in repairs depending on the issue. When buying a home, finding a house at the top of a hill can help reduce the risk of standing water in your basement, but even then, there are no guarantees. For this reason, investigating your home for potential water issues before purchasing is a must.

Sump Pump Awareness

Now, sump pumps are pretty much a standard fixture in new home builds. Having worked for a company that installed internet cables and outlets in new build houses, I don't remember ever seeing a new build that didn't include a sump pump in the basement. Consequently, just because a house comes with a sump pump doesn't mean there are (or aren't) water issues. While you're joining the house inspector you hire on the house inspection (something I HIGHLY recommend you do), listen to see if the sump pump turns on while you are there. Stay aware of how often it turns on while you are there and what the weather is doing outside at the time. Likewise, be mindful of the weather that has transpired during the previous week. If it's been raining cats and dogs for days, a running sump pump is understandable. If your area has been experiencing near-drought conditions, a running sump pump could mean there is a water issue somewhere.

The home I grew up in had no sump pump (built prior to 1920). When we were inundated with rain, we'd get some minor flooding in the basement as we were higher in elevation than the rest of the street. I think that helped tremendously. The home I own as an adult has a sump pump that goes off when we get hit with a lot of rain. I find the sump pump goes off when we run a faucet for a long time. We are in a relatively flat area so there is not much of an incline, and the ground doesn't drain water well as the soil in our area is a heavy, clay-loam. As for the sump pump, the previous owners built an enclosure around the device, which muffled/silenced the noise tremendously. That alone indicated to me that the sump pump was quite active (first time I ever saw such an enclosure). So, if you are buying a house with a sump pump, ask the owners about when it was last replaced and how often does it run. Additionally, ask them if they have had water issues in the basement.

All this said, I didn't need to even hear the sump pump to activate during the inspection or see the enclosure to know the house had water issues.

The Signs of Water Problems

Exploring the basement as a buyer, while tagging along with a house inspector, was a unique experience. First, there was a plastic trough or gutter, positioned about two inches off the ground, which ran along half of the basement walls. Given the staining in this gutter, it was clear the device was to collect water and channel it to the sump pump. Did I just buy a money pit? Turns out, the previous owner had a lot of turtles that spent time in the basement during the winter. The trough/gutter helped in getting water from turtle tanks (and relevant handling) to the sump pump. It wasn't a device to deal with a water issue with the house's structure. Still, I looked for water issues needing to be addressed.

There were indications of water seepage in a few places as we discovered minimal stains here and there on drywall where it touched the basement floor. Nothing looked alarming though. Having done some research into how homeowners hide water damage, I knew to look out for fresh paintings of walls and floors, especially in basements. The basement's laundry room floor appeared to have been painted in recent years, but it was already fading in some spots. Now, nearly 20 years living in the house, that area of the basement floor does see some minor pooling of water during huge rain events. As for the main open area of the basement, it was covered wall to wall with a thin, well-worn, carpet which showed no evidence of water damage. We removed that carpet after the entire basement flooded after a massive storm when power went out and the sump pump was offline. Aside from that instance, most of the basement flooring remains dry, even during the soggiest of times.

Now, like I mentioned, I went through the home inspection with our hired inspector. I asked him about the gutter system and other system. As I recall, he was not convinced there was any significant water issue due to flooding caused by rain or snowmelt. He was good and providing insight on ways sellers 'hide' such problems (fresh paint and new drywall the biggest concerns). Ask you inspector what to look for (and what they look for). For some ideas, check for the following:

- Mold growth on wood, drywall or other surfaces in the basement.
- A humid basement environment
- Wood, especially wall framing touching the ground, located in the basement
- Bulging areas in drywall that may be soaking up water
- The sight and/or sound of leaking pipes

- A damaged roof (which could lead to water flowing down to the basement)
- Water stains on the tiles, drywall or exposed beams that make up the basement's ceiling

Plumbing

Plumbing can be a nightmare for homeowners. True, you can prevent problems through a careful inspection of the house before buying (to prepare for upgrades needed), but Time always finds a way to make plumbing systems and fixtures fail. Again, your home inspector's assessment of the house's plumbing system is huge. Ask the inspector the following:

- Does the inspector have any major plumbing concerns?
- What plumbing upgrades would the inspector recommend IF you buy the house?
- Do all the water shutoffs work properly?
- Where are the plumbing shutoffs for the house and every plumbing fixture inside the house (sinks, toilets, bathtubs/showers, and anything else)?
- Should any shutoffs be replaced in the near-term?
- Is there any indication of mold buildup near tubs, sinks, or other water fixtures?

- Should you upgrade or replace the toilets' plumbing parts in the near-term?
- Do the toilets and faucets work properly, or is the inspector concerned about any of the fixtures?

A thorough check of all water fixtures and their related shutoff valves is crucial for preventing immediate and long-term water problems. Now, before you've purchased a potential "money pit," is the time to investigate this. Why? If the inspector recommends any upgrades, you could request the home's seller make the upgrades or drop the selling price of the home.

Chapter 5: Your Roof

As a home owner who has replaced the roofs of both a house and a garage, I can tell you that such replacements are often the most expensive home repair projects ever. The average lifespan of a roof depends on multiple factors including the type of shingles used (asphalt, metal, clay, etc.) and the annual weather conditions (snow, intense rains/hurricanes, winds, and/or drought). With the typical asphalt shingles, you're looking at an average lifespan of 20-25 years (according to the company I hired). So, I recommend you look for homes that have roofs no more than 10-13 years old. Any older and you should be seeking a reduced price for the home.

Now, I am not a roofing contractor. The problem is, many home inspectors aren't roofing contractors either. For that reason, I recommend home buyers hire a roofer to inspect the roof of any house they plan to purchase (in addition to the home inspectors check of the roof). Some roofs are estimated to last upwards of 30-35 years. A roofing contractor or specialist should be able to provide a good estimate of how many years left a roof likely has before it needs to be replaced. As an fyi, a new roof will often cost upwards of $15,000 to $20,000. We replaced our roof for under $12,000 in 2022, and that price included two new replacement skylights and new gutters. Now, when speaking with a roofing inspector (and/or the home inspector), here are some questions to ask:

- How soon does the inspector think the roof will need to be replaced?
- How many roof levels are there? This becomes an issue as contractors sometimes simply add another layer or wood to an existing roof instead of doing a complete tear-off. This leads to a lot of additional weight on the roof and could lessen the lifespan of the roof.
- Are the shingles in good condition?
- Where does the inspector suspect any water damage from previous rains/storms?
- Where does the inspector suspect any ice dams may develop?
- Does the chimney need 'repointing' (mortar repair) or any other repair/updating?
- Does the inspector have any gutter concerns?
- Does it look like the current roof was installed poorly? If yes, in what ways?
- Do any existing skylights cause the inspector any concerns (especially signs of leakage)?

Given the cost of a new roof and the hazards a damaged roof pose for a home's interior and overall structural stability, I highly recommend you take great care with regards to this portion of a home inspection. Now, I included questions pertaining to gutters and skylights, because these often are areas where water leaks occur. Make sure your inspector carefully inspects both for signs of leaks or damage. For the record, I hate skylights as they make it harder to rake snow off my roof in winter, which at times leads to ice dams. As for the new gutters we recently put on the house, it's amazing what a new or well-functioning gutter system does for keeping water out of and away from your home.

Windows and Siding

Windows and siding help protect your house from weather similarly to a roof by keeping water and the elements at bay. Damage to siding or windows can be indicative of a roof leak. As such, make sure your inspector thoroughly investigates the condition of windows and siding. Look especially for any places where an animal has entered or could enter the home. Mice and bats only need tiny gaps between siding and roofs to enter… and they can be a homeowner's worst nightmare. While you are having windows inspected, have the window seals checked over twice. Seals can be an easy fix, but you want to know what seals need replacing before a leak occurs.

Chapter 6: The Question About the Appliances

What happens to the appliances when you buy and move into a house? The answer is... it depends. Some home sellers will include the appliances, oftentimes making it a selling point (that they are including a number of 'newer' appliances with the home). Sometimes, the home seller plans to take any appliance (or some appliances) that are not 'built into' the home when they vacate the property. Find out the home seller's plans before buying the home. Why? Because, you need to know what's coming with the house and what appliances will need to be purchased (and budgeted for). You don't want to buy the home, get the keys, and then show up wanting to wash clothes only to find there is no washing machine.

Now, if the seller plans to leave the appliances in place, including them in the sale, it is possible the sale price of the home was jacked up to account for the appliances. Trouble is, sometimes the appliances aren't worth a dime and are in fact on their last legs. Imagine the seller leaves behind a stove, increasing the home's price to account for that appliance remaining. Then, after a week of use, the stove breaks down and requires a couple hundred dollars to repair. When all is said and done, you need to spend a lot to fix it or spend a lot for the heavy appliance to be removed BEFORE spending more money to buy a new (or used) stove.

I purchased my home fully equipped with the seller's appliances; he left everything behind and included them in the sale. Twenty years later, the washing machine and microwave oven are both still working well while we got many years out of the refrigerator, the dryer, and the dishwasher before having to replace them. Honestly, I wasn't real focused on the appliances when the inspector was checking the house over. Thankfully, the inspector was. He tested every appliance and provided me with estimates on how long each appliance should last. Our inspector found everything running in tip top shape; he had no concerns. When your inspector goes through the house you are buying, have them check each appliance. Ask the inspector the following:

- Are the appliances running well?
- Does the inspector have any concerns about any of the appliances?
- Does the inspector advise replacing any of the appliances in the near term (the next 6 months)?
- How long does the inspector believe the appliances will last for (on average)?

Be mindful that an inspector would not be realistically able to know if there is a wire, a belt, or some other mechanical part somewhere in an appliance that is about to give out. That said, a trained inspector will likely be able to provide a good estimate as to how long each appliance should last. If the appliances are old and appear to be nearing their end, speak with your real estate agent to see about getting the price of the house lowered.

Utility Connections

Hold on. We're not done discussing appliances. Some homes were built over a century ago, before the availability of modern conveniences, including appliances. To add to this conundrum is the issue that states are now starting to look at banning the use of certain fuel sources in new builds (with an added potential for a future struggle to obtain gas appliances). Resistance to such developments may yet stop governments from enacting or being able to enforce such building regulations. That said, I feel home buyers need to be mindful of such developments. When inspecting the home you are hoping to purchase, make sure there are adequate connections available for modern appliances. This includes the following considerations:

- **Stove** – outlets to suit stove connections of gas and electric.
- **Dishwasher** – Suitable water line and drain for the device. Also check to see if there is a water shutoff for the dishwasher.
- **Refrigerator** - Suitable electrical power outlet as well as a water line for any icemaker that is part of the fridge.
- **Washing Machine** – A water shutoff for the appliance as well as an updated electrical outlet for the appliance. Additionally, check to make certain there is a sufficient tub or sink that the machine can drain into.
- **Dryer** – check for both a gas and electric hookup for use with either power source. Additionally, make certain there is an appropriate and unblocked exhaust hose that sends dryer exhaust outside to prevent carbon monoxide from entering the home.

Ask the inspector if all appliance connections are up to code. This includes having the inspector check over an unused connection (a gas connection next to a dryer but the dryer is electric). Checking all these connections is important as you may decide to switch from gas to electric in the future or vice versa. Also, as I mentioned before, some municipalities are looking to legislate a ban on gas appliances. If this happens and all homes are required to switch to electric five years down the road, you will want to have a suitable electrical outlet available when you buy the home. If such a connection is not there, you would be required to pay an electrician to install an outlet in the future, which can be a costly expense.

Chapter 7: Where are the Buried Utility Lines?

The house we bought came with an aboveground pool that included a gas heater. The problem was, the pool was located about fifty feet back from the house. As the pool and the gas heater were so far from the house and street, the previous owner needed to have a gas line installed to reach out all the way to the pool. My one neighbor remembered when the gas line was installed. It sounds as if the gas line went all over the place due to the amount of trees and the turtle pound located between the house and the pool. Additionally, an electric line ran from the house to the pool, and I received no information regarding the placement of either of those utility lines.

Now, I am sure most people are aware that utility companies can check over a property to find buried electric wires and gas lines. Any lines installed by utility companies or municipalities should be easy for them to discover and map out for the new homeowner. But what about the gas lines and electrical wires put in place by a previous owner? I imagine utility companies can find most if not all such utility lines buried in a yard. However, what if something is missed? Before buying a home, I advise all buyers to ask the seller about any utility lines that are buried in the front, back, or side yards. True, the seller may not be aware of utility lines buried before they owned the house. Yet, their feedback could prevent you from accidentally digging up a gas line and causing an explosion resulting in injuries, or worse. If informed of any such buried utilities, make note of it and then have a utility company search for and mark utility lines, making them aware of the information you received from the seller.

Leave it to the Professionals

This is just a concern of mine… utility lines being installed by amateurs. Just don't! If you need to put in a gas line or electrical wiring, I recommend everyone hire the professionals to do the job. Mishaps with utilities can be deadly, so be careful.

Chapter 8: What are the Passcodes and How are They Changed?

This chapter likely seems self-explanatory, but I still feel a few added notes are worth discussing. Yes, many homes have one or more passcodes (security system passwords) used daily to allow access to different parts of the property. The main house, the garage, a gate, a shed, and who knows what else may be equipped with a security system that requires inputting a passcode before entering. First things first, ask the seller or their agent/representative (after you take possession of the house) what doors, gates, or structures have security systems and require a passcode for shutting down the security system. Then ask for the passcode(s) and how you can change the passcode. Ask for all manuals and the contact information for the companies that installed and service the security systems. THEN GO AND IMMEDIATELY CHANGE THE PASSCODES!

I'm sure the seller is a good person as is the seller's family and friends and neighbors. Yet, do you want to risk it? Change the exterior locks to ALL doors while you're at it! Make these changes BEFORE you move in any furniture or other items into the house. Now, I'm not an insurance agent, but I wonder if changing passcodes and door locks is required to be covered by insurance. If it's not, it ought to be. If the technology and reprogramming the passcodes are too complicated, at least change the door locks. As for figuring out the security system, contact the company that installed the system for help in changing the passcodes.

Chapter 9: Where are the manuals?

The couple we bought our house from was amazing is so many things they did. I'm sure they were just being thorough for their own sakes, but their efforts made things easier for my wife and me. This is especially true of the binder full of manuals they kept, which they left for us at the home when we moved in. We are talking manuals for every major appliance from the refrigerator and dishwasher to the washer and dryer. They even kept the owner's manual for the pool heater and the riding lawn mower. These manuals are incredible for providing instructions on how to deal with "what if" scenarios in cases where an appliance stops working. We are talking how to add new belts, bulbs, fans, and other parts that will need to be changed routinely due to normal wear and tear. What's more, manuals usually contain part numbers and the serial number for the specific appliance that is in your new home. Believe me, whether you repair an appliance on your own or you hire a technician, having the manuals with serial and part numbers is critical to ensure repairs are done right and with the right replacement parts.

No Manuals? No Problem

It is likely that the seller of your new home did not keep all or even many of the owner's manuals for all the appliances you are about to inherit. If this is the case, I recommend you go online and find/download digital copies of the owner's manuals for all appliances in the house you just purchased. It's probably too costly and unnecessary to print out the complete manuals. However, it would be a wise decision to print out the appliance's serial number, replacement parts listing, and the 'what to do if broken' sections of the owner's manuals. Then, put those manuals in a binder and store them in a safe space. Those manuals come in mighty handy when an appliance breaks down.

Chapter 10: Are there any hidden spaces?

About 6 months after moving into the house we found a nice little surprise. To be honest, it wasn't a big deal, but it was a surprise and a minor headache. We found a crawl space in the upstairs bathroom. The only real 'issue' besides a couple boxes filled with crap we had to throw out was that the exhaust fan for the bathroom didn't actually filter air to the outside. For this reason, I recommend every homebuyer ask the seller about what, if any, hidden crawl spaces exist. On the positive side of things, you may find out about some hidden storage spaces that will make life a whole lot easier down the road. On the negative side, there may be a hidden space where a previous owner, not necessarily the seller you purchased the house from, dumped a huge stack of very old and nail-filled 2x4s. That's at least what my brother and I found at our family home when we removed an old wall.

Now, for a fun (or scary) research project, do a search online for hidden rooms and crawl spaces that people discovered in homes they purchased. Spend an hour or two looking up these discoveries. Some people find hidden treasures, usually in the form of antique furniture that is worth a good amount of money. Others, like my brother and me, find a room filled with garbage that ranges from 'a little dirty' to 'absolutely disgusting' in nature. This research you complete will make it clear why you want to know about crawl spaces and hidden rooms prior to taking ownership of a home.

The Discovery Channel in Your House

I'm an archaeologist, so searching for things is exhilarating and a part of my daily life. That said, here is a little recommendation. After purchasing a home, spend a day searching the house top to bottom. Look in crawl spaces, attics, the garage, and anywhere else. Why? People often leave stuff behind. Some just forget about things while others just don't want to take things with them after selling their home. Aside from a dead television and a recliner covered in cat hair, I found an antique Carpenter's plane, which now hangs in my workshop. Other gems included a gigantic fish tank and other antique tools. I haven't found a $100,000 stash of pennies, but I did get some cool things. Take a look around and see what's there.

Chapter 11: What's Up with the Driveway and Awning?

I know that's a weird combination of things to throw into a chapter title, but it is for a good reason. Both driveways and awnings come with intricate necessities for maintenance and COULD include an already agreed upon service contract with a company or contractor. Let's dive in.

Driveway Maintenance

I grew up and purchased my current home in the Buffalo, New York area. That translates to long winters with LOTS of snow. In the almost 20 years at our house, we've been hit with 6.5 feet over a couple days and then twice where we were covered by 4-5 feet of snow over the course of a couple days. Did I mention my driveway is 80 feet long? Anyway, I asked NO questions when I purchased my home. None. Nada. Big mistake. In an area fraught with weather issues, I should have asked:

- Are we in a snow belt area? Do we get a ton of snow?
- Do areas of the driveway (or property) get a lot of standing water during heavy rainstorms?

From there, it's time to ask maintenance questions:

- When was the driveway last treated/serviced? Blacktop driveways generally need to be resealed every other year.
- What company sealed the driveway? If the sealing job was done poorly, that company should be avoided in the future. If the company did an exceptional job, it would be great to know who they are and get future quotes from that company.
- When was the driveway put in?
- What company put the driveway in? Again, a poor job tells you which companies to avoid.
- What problems or maintenance issues should I be aware of with the driveway?

Okay. The last question is a stretch. Why? Because the home seller could screw themselves with an honest answer. That said, it's good to know what you're getting into. My driveway, thankfully, has been pretty solid throughout the 20 years. I wish I asked the seller/previous owner who they had resealed the driveway and who installed it. Such answers would have helped me track down dependable companies for repairs I did. For the record, some companies are not good at servicing driveways. There are scammers everywhere. If the seller doesn't provide detailed answers to the above questions, talk to the neighbors. Do they know of any problems the seller had with the driveway? Admittedly, they may not say anything until you've purchased the property, but their input can aid you in maintaining the driveway.

As for the winter issues, I wish I had asked the seller how they managed the snow. Did he hire a snow plow company or use a snow blower? If he used a snow blower, how powerful was the snow blower? Believe me, there's a huge difference between a 6 horsepower snow blower and an 8 horse power snow blower. I ended up playing things by ear. As an archaeologist, shoveling is my go-to. But 80 feet of driveway? My godfather got me a used Ariens snow blower, a wonderful surprise. It was about 6 horsepower and did a great job. We get heavy, lake-effect snow, which requires a lot of horsepower to clear. I ultimately purchased a new 7.5-8 horsepower snow blower which is great at managing the driveway and Buffalo's snowstorms. That said, I wish I had asked more about the driveway and how the previous owner managed the driveway during snowstorms.

As for contracts and plow services (or even resealing services), ask the seller if there are any contracts they have in place. If there are, get details and see about stopping the services if you don't want them. From my experience, contracts for driveway maintenance have to be renewed each year. Just the same, check into it. Awnings and related maintenance contracts are totally different.

Awning Maintenance

I admit it openly and freely. My wife is better at details than I am. Our home came with an awning, which covered a good portion of the back deck. One fine September day after our first summer of owning the house, I came home to find the awning gone. What the hell?! I loved the awning and sitting out on the deck. What the heck happened? When my wife got home she was not really all that surprised. Apparently, the previous owner of the home had a contract with a company that would take down, clean, and store the awning for the winter months. I had no recollection of that from any discussions we had with the previous owner or the realtor. Now, just shy of 20 years later, I am grateful for the company and happy to spend the money to have the awning removed and stored. Yet, what if my wife and I could not afford such a service? I imagine we could tell the company, who left a bill for their removing the awning, that we did not have a contract with them. However, it seems easier to just go in knowing about any such contracts ahead of time. Also, for those who want to manage an awning on their own, that means storing an awning (keeping it wrinkle-free) and washing/cleaning the awning. Cleaning is usually an additional charge, but it is definitely worth it as far as I am concerned. As an FYI, I purchased a 10'x10' pop-up awning I use when our main awning is in storage so I can have an awning available anytime.

Chapter 12: What is the Weather Like?

As previously mentioned, I purchased a home in the Buffalo, New York region. So, when I was looking for a home, it seems a no-brainer that I could expect any home I purchased to get pummeled by snow throughout the winter months. Right? Wrong.

Buffalo, like many places throughout North America, is impacted by a variety of elements, especially the great lake (Erie) that sits west of the metropolitan area. You've heard of Buffalo's "lake-effect" snowstorms, right? Anyway, the lake helps create a lot of 'micro' climates, which means there are big differences in weather between even two western New York towns that border each other. Towns south of Buffalo get the majority of the snow while Buffalo and the towns to its north get significantly less over the winter months. For example, most storms might dump 6 inches to a foot of snow on the southtowns while Buffalo and the northtowns get 2-3 inches. That's a huge difference. Now, here's where things get interesting. I learned that one town in particular borders the towns to the north and south in a way that when bands of lake-effect snow move, this one town has a tendency to get pummeled no matter where a snowstorm focuses its strength. Yeah, that's the town I of course purchased a home in.

Here are questions I should have asked the person selling the home I ultimately bought:

- What range of weather does the house usually get?
- What are the biggest weather concerns I will have during a typical year?
- What was the worst storm you ever experience while living in this house?
- What was the biggest damage the house ever received from a storm?
- Is there an area of the roof that develops ice dams during the winter?
- Does the area get a lot of tornados and/or hurricanes?
- Is the area often impacted by wildfires?
- Is flooding ever an issue for the home?
- Should I get flood insurance?

Now, during the last 20 years, I have had to manage a snowstorm where I received 6.5 feet of snow, which I had to have removed from my roof by a contractor. I would say that is the worst weather experience yet. On two other occasions we got hit with storms dropping 4-5 feet of snow over a couple days. As bad as that is, our region rarely gets impacted by hurricanes, which I am quite happy with. Tornados are likewise rare. The point is, find out what potential extremes in weather you could be facing. In addition to the house's seller, ask your realtor and new neighbors the same questions.

Chapter 13: How Old Are the Windows?

They say that "eyes are the windows to the soul" and what not. Yeah, well windows on a house are vacuums that drain homes of conditioned air. Anyway, whether you heat air in the winter or cool air in the summer, crappy windows will lead to super high energy bills. Period. Window efficiency is the name of the game, and many homes on the market, in turn, have NO GAME!

My family home was built in the early 1900s (Pre-1910). Translation... the frigid winds of Buffalo winters whipped through the windows like they weren't even there. The solution my parents adopted was to tape plastic sheeting over the windows for the season. That helped, but it wasn't perfect. They ultimately saved enough to replace the windows, which in turn significantly helped lower heating costs. When you consider that most first-time homebuyers are young and just starting out in adulthood, few have the money to waste heating a home that is doing nothing but heating the outdoors. This is a major concern for all.

When buying a home, find out how old the windows are. Oftentimes, the realtor will have a list of when the house received structural and appliance updates, including windows. If the realtor doesn't know, ask your inspector to give you an estimate. Any windows installed pre-1990s is troublesome as far as I am concerned. True, windows made before 1990 could have been upgraded in some way or the owner may have had a great contractor insulate the heck out of the windows thereby cutting off heat (or cooled air) loss. You need to determine if that is the case or if the windows are just old and inefficient with regards to air conditioning.

Here's the thing, utility bills (electric and gas especially) are two of the biggest bills families pay each month. We are talking a couple hundred dollars to several hundred dollars a month in costs, depending on the season. Making certain you know what you are signing up for, window-wise, before you buy a house, can save you a great deal of grief and money in the long run. Here are the things I recommend asking a realtor or home seller about a house you are seeking to buy:

- How old are the windows? Even a ball park number like "pre-1975" can make a huge difference in negotiating the final price you purchase a house for.
- What brand of windows are they? Some of the costlier brands warrant the higher costs due to how well they keep in heated and/or cooled air).

- Have the windows' surrounding insulation been updated in recent years? If yes, in what way?
- Has an 'energy audit' been performed on the house? If yes, were recommendations provided by the audit implemented? What specifically was done after the audit to increase the efficiency of airflow in the home? An energy audit essentially finds where air is leaking, which in turn leads to increased utility costs.

This is when hiring your own realtor is especially important. If it turns out the windows are ancient and do next to nothing keeping out cold air (and keeping warm air in), discuss how to negotiate the house price. Arguing that the windows would need to be replaced in a relatively short amount of time could be a huge bargaining chip. Again, work with YOUR real estate agent/realtor on deciding how to proceed and if the windows are worth the negotiating.

By the way, I recommend getting windows replaced as soon as possible if they are old and/or inefficient. I also advise you get an energy audit done as soon as possible to see what other "inefficiencies" exist and are costing you money.

Chapter 14: Concluding Thoughts

There's my 2 cents regarding "things I wish I had asked" when buying my home. Frankly, I recommend everyone consider what's listed here AND ask family and friends for what questions they wish they'd asked when buying a home. That said, here's the real tip worth considering.

Hiring a realtor at times seems like a waste of money. I mean, it's easy enough to search newspapers or the internet for available homes. There are certainly enough search engines available that will help you locate homes with all or most of the features you want, homes in just about every zip code. That's what my wife and I did. Welp, when we found the home we wanted to buy, we were looking at the prospect of negotiating the sale price without any support while the seller had a realtor/real estate agent assisting. Now, looking back, my wife and I are so grateful we decided to hire a realtor for the negotiations for purchasing what has been our home for almost 2 decades. The realtor's input helped us get a lower price while keeping us from making bids that would have likely cost us the opportunity to buy. Furthermore, as I discussed throughout this book, a realtor/real estate agent can provide insights and guidance that could save you thousands of dollars in the near term and tens of thousands down the road. Bottom line, I strongly advise you hire a realtor.

Now, go find your home. I hope my advice and guidance helps you find a home and negotiate a great price. I also hope you will share with others what you learn from this book and from your own adventures in house shopping. It can be a nerve-racking experience to say the least, but it's an effort that can lead you to your own paradise as long as if you're careful and take time to do some research. Wishing you all the best.